T0417993

THE INDIAN OCEAN TSUNAMI

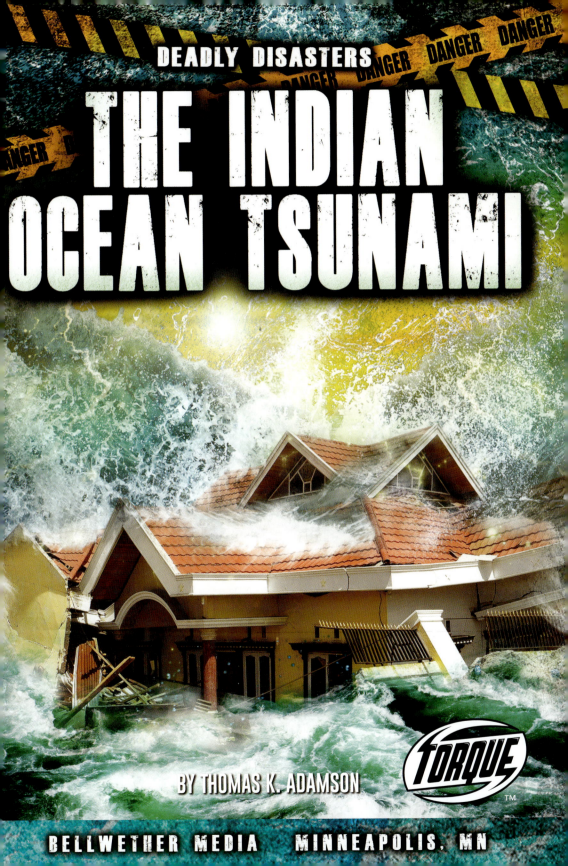

BY THOMAS K. ADAMSON

BELLWETHER MEDIA · MINNEAPOLIS, MN

™

Torque brims with excitement perfect for thrill-seekers of all kinds. Discover daring survival skills, explore uncharted worlds, and marvel at mighty engines and extreme sports. In *Torque* books, anything can happen. Are you ready?

This edition first published in 2022 by Bellwether Media, Inc.

No part of this publication may be reproduced in whole or in part without written permission of the publisher. For information regarding permission, write to Bellwether Media, Inc., Attention: Permissions Department, 6012 Blue Circle Drive, Minnetonka, MN 55343.

Library of Congress Cataloging-in-Publication Data

Names: Adamson, Thomas K., 1970- author.
Title: The Indian Ocean tsunami / by Thomas K. Adamson.
Description: Minneapolis, MN : Bellwether Media, Inc., 2022. | Series: Deadly disasters | Includes bibliographical references and index. | Audience: Ages 7-12 | Audience: Grades 4-6 | Summary: "Amazing photography accompanies engaging information about the Indian Ocean Tsunami. The combination of high-interest subject matter and light text is intended for students in grades 3 through 7"– Provided by publisher.

Identifiers: LCCN 2021020932 (print) | LCCN 2021020933 (ebook) | ISBN 9781644875308 (library binding) | ISBN 9781648344381 (ebook)
Subjects: LCSH: Indian Ocean Tsunami, 2004–Juvenile literature. | Tsunamis–Indian Ocean–Juvenile literature. | Earthquakes–Indian Ocean–Juvenile literature.
Classification: LCC GC221.5 .A427 2022 (print) | LCC GC221.5 (ebook) | DDC 363.34/94091824090511–dc23
LC record available at https://lccn.loc.gov/2021020932
LC ebook record available at https://lccn.loc.gov/2021020933

Editor: Kieran Downs   Designer: Josh Brink

Printed in the United States of America, North Mankato, MN.

TABLE OF CONTENTS

CAUTION

STRANGE SIGHTS AT THE BEACH

Simon Lee took photos with his wife and children on Patong Beach, Thailand. Suddenly, the water **receded**. Fish flopped on the wet sand.

Simon called for his family to run away from the beach. In minutes, fast-moving ocean water rushed ashore. Simon and his family escaped to a balcony. His fast thinking saved their lives!

HARBOR WAVE

In Japanese, *tsunami* means "harbor wave."

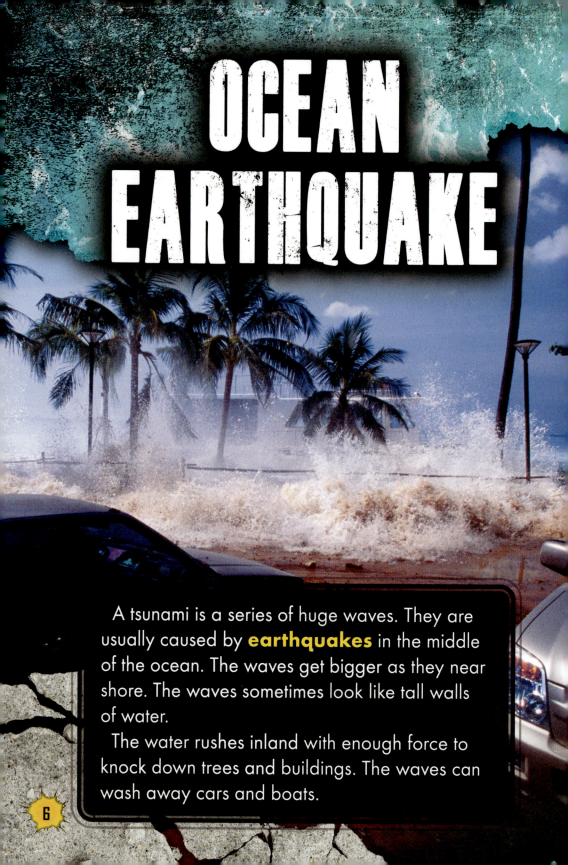

OCEAN EARTHQUAKE

A tsunami is a series of huge waves. They are usually caused by **earthquakes** in the middle of the ocean. The waves get bigger as they near shore. The waves sometimes look like tall walls of water.

The water rushes inland with enough force to knock down trees and buildings. The waves can wash away cars and boats.

HOW A TSUNAMI BEGINS

WAVES ARE SHORTER AND FARTHER APART NEAR EARTHQUAKE

EARTHQUAKE

WAVES ARE TALLER AND CLOSER TOGETHER NEAR SHORE

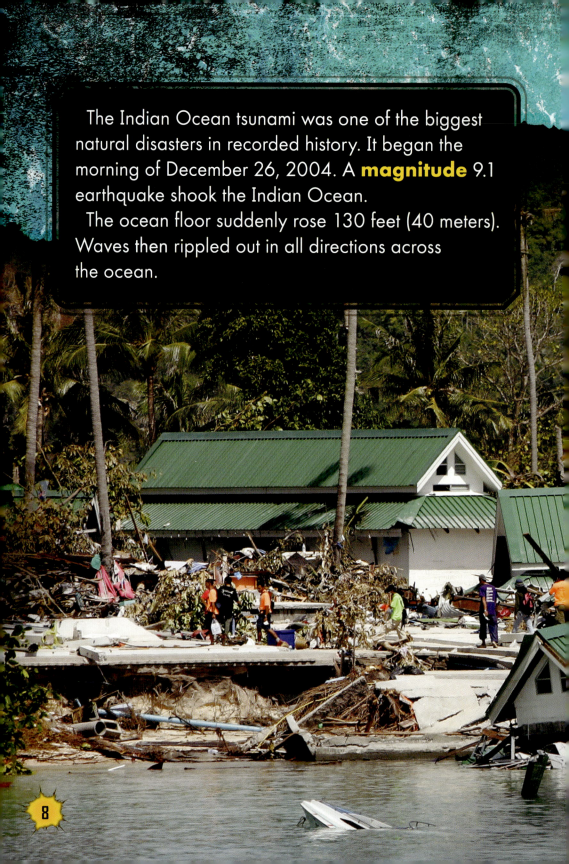

The Indian Ocean tsunami was one of the biggest natural disasters in recorded history. It began the morning of December 26, 2004. A **magnitude** 9.1 earthquake shook the Indian Ocean.

The ocean floor suddenly rose 130 feet (40 meters). Waves then rippled out in all directions across the ocean.

A MIGHTY JOLT

The earthquake that caused the tsunami was the third most powerful earthquake ever recorded.

In just 30 minutes, the first waves hit Banda Aceh, Indonesia. In some places, the waves were 100 feet (30 meters) high.

Waves soon hit Thailand, Sri Lanka, and India. Large waves even crashed into Africa, 5,000 miles (8,000 kilometers) away. People there did not know about the earthquake on the other side of the ocean.

TSUNAMI DAMAGE IN SRI LANKA

AREAS AFFECTED

BANGLADESH

MYANMAR
(BURMA)

INDIA

THAILAND

SOMALIA

MALAYSIA

KENYA

TANZANIA

MOZAMBIQUE

SRI LANKA

INDONESIA

AUSTRALIA

MADAGASCAR

AREAS AFFECTED =

AMAZINGLY FAST WAVES

Tsunami waves can speed across
the ocean at about 500 miles
(805 kilometers) per hour!

POWERFUL WAVES

The first warning of disaster came when the ocean receded. Many people did not know about tsunami dangers. They curiously watched the strange sight. Some people went out to the beach to pick up stranded fish.

But then the water came back and rushed onto the shore. People on the beach had no time to run to high ground.

TIMELINE

AROUND 8:30 A.M. WIB

A giant tsunami wave hits Banda Aceh, Indonesia

7:58 A.M. INDONESIA TIME (WIB)

A magnitude 9.1 earthquake occurs in the Indian Ocean, near the coast of Sumatra, Indonesia

AROUND 9:30 A.M. WIB

The tsunami reaches Thailand

AROUND 4:00 P.M. WIB (12:00 P.M. LOCAL TIME)

Waves make it all the way across the Indian Ocean to the African countries of Somalia, Kenya, Tanzania, Madagascar, and Mozambique

AROUND 10:00 A.M. WIB (8:00 A.M. LOCAL TIME)

Tsunami waves hit Sri Lanka and India

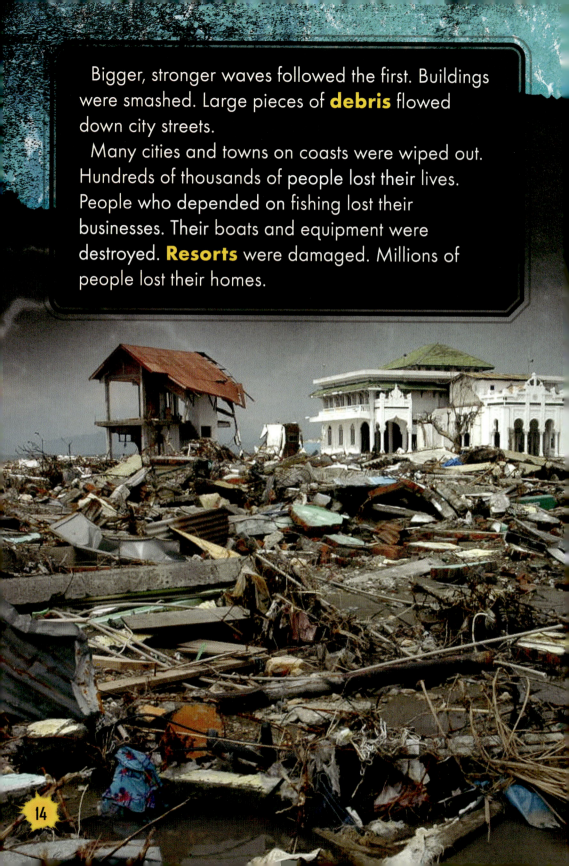

Bigger, stronger waves followed the first. Buildings were smashed. Large pieces of **debris** flowed down city streets.

Many cities and towns on coasts were wiped out. Hundreds of thousands of people lost their lives. People who depended on fishing lost their businesses. Their boats and equipment were destroyed. **Resorts** were damaged. Millions of people lost their homes.

WAVE ARRIVAL TIMES

THAILAND

INDIA

SOMALIA

SRI LANKA

KENYA

2 hours after
earthquake

INDONESIA

MADAGASCAR

4 hours after
earthquake

TANZANIA

EARTHQUAKE

6 hours after
earthquake

8 hours after
earthquake

AUSTRALIA

10 hours after
earthquake

SHIP WRECKED

The tsunami carried boats far inland.
One large ship was carried 5 miles
(8 kilometers) from the coast!

THE WORLD HELPS

The tsunami surprised the world. News outlets showed the damage. People around the world **donated** money to help. **Relief agencies** raised an estimated $14 billion.

Many roads were damaged. People in remote areas could not travel. Military aircraft brought in supplies. In some places, only helicopters were able to land.

RELIEF AGENCY

The tsunami damaged water sources. This can lead to disease. Relief agencies made sure the water supply was safe. They also brought food, clothing, and medicine to survivors.

The relief agencies built many **temporary** homes. They rebuilt roads and schools. But it took years to completely rebuild.

PRESIDENTIAL HELP

Former U.S. presidents George H.W. Bush and Bill Clinton worked together to raise money to help people affected by the tsunami.

PREPARING FOR A TSUNAMI

TSUNAMI WARNING SYSTEM

In 2004, the Indian Ocean had no working tsunami warning system. **Sensors** on the seafloor now measure earthquake movement. People know when to watch for tsunamis. New **shelters** have open ground floors. Water can rush through instead of causing damage.

Big tsunamis do not happen often. But scientists are still learning about how to be safe from tsunami waves!

PREPARATION KIT

FIRST AID KIT

FOOD AND DRINKING WATER

RADIO

FLASHLIGHT

BLANKETS

CELL PHONE CHARGERS

GLOSSARY

debris—the junk or pieces left behind when something is destroyed

donated—gave something to help others in need

earthquakes—sudden, violent shakings of the earth that may cause damage

magnitude—the power of an earthquake

receded—moved back

relief agencies—organizations that help people in need

resorts—places where people go for rest and relaxation

sensors—scientific instruments that can measure changes

shelters—places that offer protection from bad weather or danger

temporary—lasting for a limited period of time

TO LEARN MORE

AT THE LIBRARY

Farndon, John. *Extreme Earthquakes and Tsunamis*. Minneapolis, Minn.: Hungry Tomato, 2018.

Hayes, Vicki. *Surviving a Tsunami*. Minneapolis, Minn.: Kaleidoscope, 2020.

Rathburn, Betsy. *Tsunamis*. Minneapolis, Minn.: Bellwether Media, 2020.

ON THE WEB

FACTSURFER

Factsurfer.com gives you a safe, fun way to find more information.

1. Go to www.factsurfer.com

2. Enter "Indian Ocean tsunami" into the search box and click 🔍.

3. Select your book cover to see a list of related content.

CAUTION

CAUTION

INDEX

CAUTION CAUTION